Anonymous

Music for the Church Service

Responses, Chants and Tunes for Congregational and Choir Use

Anonymous

Music for the Church Service
Responses, Chants and Tunes for Congregational and Choir Use

ISBN/EAN: 9783337296759

Printed in Europe, USA, Canada, Australia, Japan

Cover: Foto ©Lupo / pixelio.de

More available books at **www.hansebooks.com**

MUSIC FOR THE CHURCH SERVICE.

Responses, Chants, and Tunes,

FOR CONGREGATIONAL AND CHOIR USE.

"Let the people praise Thee, O God;
Yea, let all the people praise Thee." — PSALM lxvii. 5.

E. P. DUTTON AND COMPANY.
BOSTON: 135 WASHINGTON STREET.
NEW YORK: 762 BROADWAY.
MDCCCLXIX.

INDEX.

RESPONSES AND CHANTS.

HYMN TUNES.

Versicles and Responses.

Thomas Tallis. 1565.

MINISTER.

ANSWER.

ORG.

O Lord, o - pen Thou our lips.

And our mouth shall show forth Thy praise.

MINISTER.

Glory be to the Father, and to the Son, and to the Holy Ghost;

ANSWER.

As it was in the beginning, is now, and ever shall be: world with - out . . end. A - MEN.

MINISTER.

ANSWER.

Praise ye the Lord.

The Lord's Name be prais - ed.

¶ *Here follow the* VENITE EXULTEMUS, *the* PSALMS FOR THE DAY, *the* LESSONS, *the* CANTICLES, *and the* APOSTLES' CREED.

MINISTER.

The Lord be with you.

ANSWER.

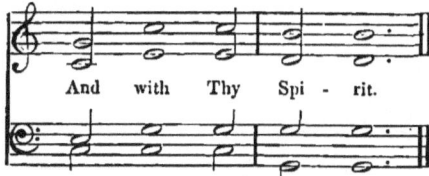

And with Thy Spi - rit.

MINISTER.

Let us pray.
O Lord, show Thy mercy up-on us.

ANSWER.

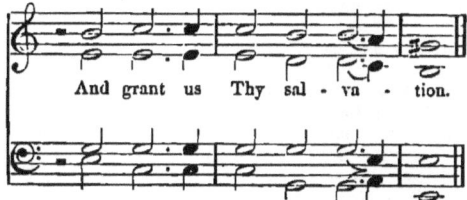

And grant us Thy sal - va - tion.

MINISTER.

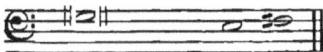

O God, make clean }
our hearts with- } in us.

ANSWER.

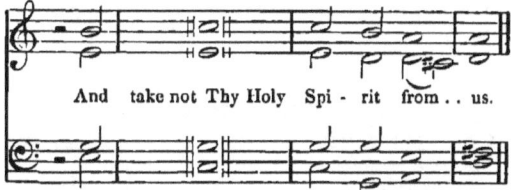

And take not Thy Holy Spi - rit from .. us.

MINISTER.   **AFTER THE COLLECTS.**   **CLOSE.**

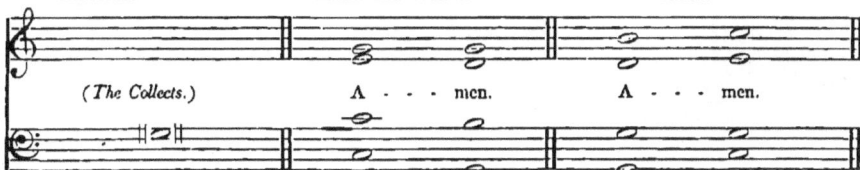

(The Collects.)   A - - - men.   A - - - men.

The Litany.

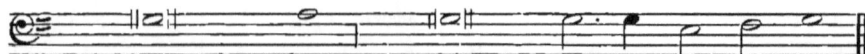

O God the Father, of   Heaven: have mercy upon us   mis - er - a - ble   sinners.

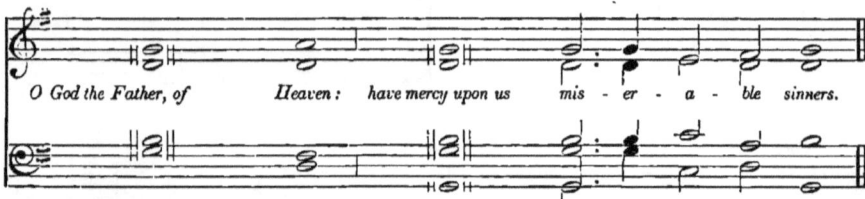

O God the Father, of   Heaven: have mercy upon us   mis - er - a - ble   sinners.

O God the Son, Redeemer of } the { world: have mercy upon us   mis - er - a - ble   sinners.

O God the Son, Redeemer of the   world: have mercy upon us   mis - er - a - ble   sinners.

O God the Holy Ghost, proceed- } ing from the Father and the { Son :   have mercy upon us   mis - er - a - ble   sinners.

O God the Holy Ghost, proceed- ing from the Father and the { Son: have mercy upon us   mis - er - a - ble   sinners.

O Holy, blessed, and glorious } Trinity, three Persons and one { God :   have mercy upon us   mis - er - a - ble   sinners.

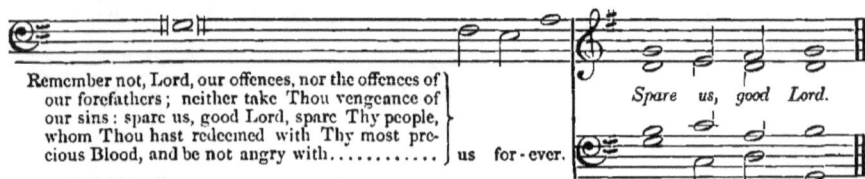

O Holy, blessed, and glorious Trinity, three Persons and one { God: have mercy upon us   mis - er - a - ble   sinners.

Remember not, Lord, our offences, nor the offences of our forefathers; neither take Thou vengeance of our sins: spare us, good Lord, spare Thy people, whom Thou hast redeemed with Thy most precious Blood, and be not angry with............ } us for - ever.   Spare us, good Lord.

From all evil and mischief; from sin, from the crafts and assaults of the devil; from Thy wrath, and from everlast- - - - - - - - - - - - } ing damnation.   Good Lord, de - liver us.†

We sinners do beseech Thee to hear us, O Lord God; and that it may please Thee to rule and govern Thy holy Church universal in .... } the right way;   We beseech } Thee to hear { us, good Lord.‡

† N. B.—This response to be repeated after the next seven Supplications.

‡ N. B. —This response to be repeated after the next fifteen Supplications.

Son of God: We beseech Thee to hear us.

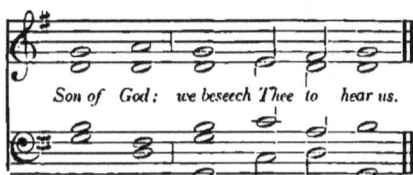

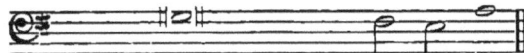

Son of God: we beseech Thee to hear us.

O Lamb of God: that takest away the sins of the world;

O Lamb of God: that takest away the sins of the world;

Grant us Thy peace.

Have mer - cy up - on us.

O Christ, hear us.

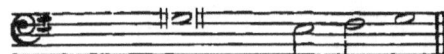

O Christ, hear us.

Lord, have mer - cy up - on us.

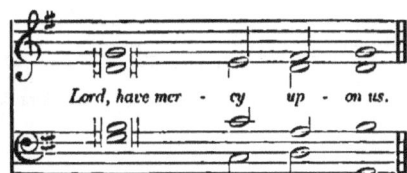

Lord, have mer - cy up - on us.

Christ, have mer - cy up - on us.
Lord, have mer - cy up - on us.

Christ, have mer - cy up - on us.
Lord, have mer - cy up - on us.

v

MINISTER AND PEOPLE.

Our Father, * * * But deliver us from evil.　　　A - men.

MINISTER.　　　　　　　　　ANSWER.

O Lord, deal not with us accord-
ing to } our sins.　　Neither reward us according to our in-i - qui - ties.

Let us pray. O God, merciful Father,* * *
through Jesus Christ. . our Lord.　　O Lord, arise, help us, and
deliver us for Thy Name's sake.

O God, we have heard,* * * in the old time be-fore them.　　O Lord, arise, help us, and deliver us
for Thine hon - our.

ANSWER.

Glory be to the Father, and to the Son: and to the Holy Ghost;..........

As it was in the begin-ning, is now, and ever shall be: world without end. A - men.

From our enemies defend us, O Christ.

Graciously look upon our af - flic - tions.

With pity behold the sorrows of our hearts.

Mercifully forgive the sins of Thy peo - ple.

Favourably with mercy hear our prayers.

O Son of David, have mercy up - on us.

Both now and ever vouchsafe to hear us, O Christ.

MIN.—O Lord, let thy mercy be showed up- on us;

Graciously hear us, O Christ; graciously hear us, O Lord Christ.

ANS.—As we do put our trust in Thee.

CLOSE.

Let us pray. * * *

A - - men.   A - - men.

The remaining Prayers and Thanksgivings to be said, and the Amens answered as before.

Communion Service.

Kyrie Eleison. (At the Decalogue.) Dr. HODGES.

Lord, have mer - cy up - on us, and in - cline our hearts to keep this law.

After the Tenth Commandment.

Lord, have mercy up - on us, and write all these Thy laws in our hearts, we be-seech Thee.

Gloria tibi, Domine.
(At the giving out of the Gospel.) TALLIS.

Glo - ry be to Thee, O Lord.

After the Gospel.

Thanks be to Thee, O Lord.

At the Offertory.

All things come of Thee, O Lord: and of Thine own have we . . . giv - en Thee.

The Nicene Creed.

SET TO THE VIIIth GREGORIAN TONE, 1st ENDING.

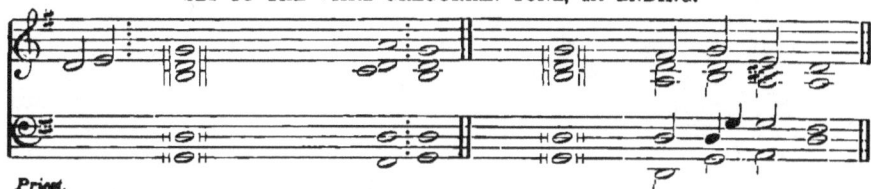

Priest.

I BE - LIEVE IN ONE GOD,	
The Father Al- - - -	might - y,
And in one Lord Jesus Christ, the only begotten Son of................	God,
God of God, Light of.....	Light,
Begotten, not made, Being of one substance with the...	Fa - ther;
Who, for us men, and for our salvation, came down from	heaven,
And was made	man,
He suffered, and was......	buri - ed;
And ascended into........	heaven,
And He shall come again with glory to judge both quick and the..........	dead;
And I believe in the Holy Ghost, the Lord and Giver of	Life,
Who with the Father and the Son together is worshipped and	glori - fied,
And I believe one Catholic and Apostolic	Church.
And I look for the Resur- rection of the	dead,

Maker of heaven and earth, and of all things visible	and in - vis - ible:		
Begotten of His Fa- ther be- - - - -	fore —	all worlds;	
Very	God of	ve - ry God,	
By	Whom all things were made;		
And was incarnate by the Holy Ghost of the	Vir - gin	Ma - ry,	
And was crucified al- so for us under....	Pon - tius	Pi - late.	
And the third day He rose again, according	to	the	Scrip - tures;
And sitteth on the right hand........	of	the	Fa - ther.
Whose kingdom ...	shall have	no	end.
Who proceedeth from the Fa - ther	and the Son,		
Who spake........	by	the	Pro - phets.
I acknowledge one Baptism for the re-	mis - sion	of	sins;
And the Life of the	world to come. A - men.		

Sanctus.

PRIEST.

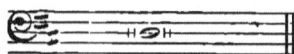

Therefore with Angels and Archangels, and with all the company of heaven, we laud and magnify Thy glorious Name; evermore praising Thee, and saying,

CHOIR.

MARBECK, 1550.

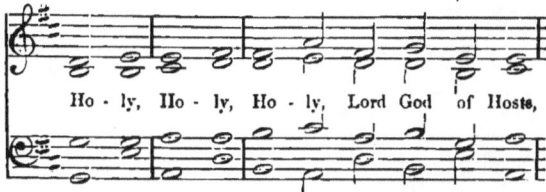

Ho - ly, Ho - ly, Ho - ly, Lord God of Hosts,

IX

SANCTUS. Concluded.

Heaven and earth are full of Thy Glo-ry: Glo-ry be to Thee, O Lord Most High. A-men.

Appropriate Hymns. Nos. 65 and 111.

Agnus Dei.

(While the Priest receives the Communion.)

From the
"MISSA DE ANGELIS."

(Three times.)

O Lamb of God, that tak-est a-way the sins of the world;

1st and 2nd time.

3d time.

Have mer - - - cy up-on us. Grant us Thy peace.

Gloria in Excelsis.

1 Glory be to ... ... God on high, and on earth... peace, good will towards men.
2 We praise Thee, we } wor-ship Thee, we glorify Thee, we give thanks to } Thee for Thy great glory,
  bless Thee, we }

9 For Thou only.... art — holy; Thou.......... on-ly art the Lord;
10 Thou only,O Christ, } art most high in }
   with the } Ho-ly Ghost, the } glory of God the Father A-men.

3 O Lord God,.......... heaven-ly King,　God the.......... Fa - ther Al - — - mighty.
4 O Lord, the only begot- ⎫
　　　　　　　ten Son, ⎰ Je - sus Christ; O Lord God, Lamb of God, Son of　the　Father,

5 That takest away the.. sins of the world. have mercy....... up - on us.
6 Thou that takest away the sins of the world, have mercy....... up - on us.
7 Thou that takest away the sins of the world, re - - - - - - ceive our prayer.
8 Thou that sittest at the ⎫
　　　　right hand of ⎰ God the　Father, have mercy....... up - on us.

D. C. verses 9 & 10. For Thou only art holy;

Nunc Dimittis.

(After the Blessing.)

Lord, now lettest Thou ⎫
　　Thy servant de- ⎰ part in peace: ac - - - - - - cord - ing to Thy word.
For mine............. eyes have seen: Thy.............. — sal - va - — - tion,
Which Thou......... hast pre - par - ed: before the face of all — peo - — - ple;
To be a Light to ...... lighten the Gen-tiles: and to be the glory of Thy peo-ple Is - ra - el.
Glory be to the Father, and to the Son: and .... to the Ho - ly Ghost;
As it was in the begin- ⎫
　　　ning, is now, and ⎰ ev - er shall be: world without ..... end. — A - — - men.

Venite, exultemus Domino.

TALLIS.

1 O come, let us sing un - to   the   Lord : let us heartily re- } joice in the .. } strength of   our   sal - vation.

2 Let us come before } His presence } with thanks-giving : and show ourselves glad   in   Him   with psalms.

3 For the Lord is a ... great — God : and a great ...... King a - bove   all   gods.

4 In His hand are all } the corners } of   the   earth : and the strength } of the....... } hills   is   His   — also.

5 The sea is His,..... and   He made it : and His hands pre- pared   the   dry   — land.

6 O come, let us wor- ship, } and   fall down : and kneel be- - - fore   the   Lord   our Maker.

7 For He is the....... Lord   our   God : and we are the } people of His }

8 O worship the Lord } in the } beauty of holiness : pasture, and the } let the whole earth stand sheep of   His   — hand. in   awe   of Him.

9 For He cometh, for } He cometh to } judge   the   earth : and with right- eousness   to } judge   the } world, and the peo - ple with His truth.

Glory be to the Father, and to the Son : and.......... .. to   the   Ho - ly Ghost,

As it was in the begin- ning, is now, and } ev - er shall be : world without.... end.   —   A - — - men.

Easter-Day.

[Instead of the VENITE EXULTEMUS DOMINO.]

1 Christ our Pass- over is sacrificed } for   —   us : therefore .... let   us   keep   the feast ;

2 Not with the old leaven, neither with the leaven of malice and .. } wick - ed - ness : but with the un- leavened bread } of sin- - - - } cer - - i - ty and truth.

3 Christ being raised from the dead, } dieth no more : death hath no } more do- - } min - ion o - ver Him.

4 For in that He died, He died unto } sin   —   once : but in that He liveth, He... } liv - eth un - to God.

5 Likewise reckon ye also yourselves to be dead indeed .. } un - to   sin : but alive unto } God through } Je - sus Christ our Lord.

6 Christ is risen...... from the   dead : and become the } first- .... } fruits of them that slept.

7 For since by .... man came death : by man came al- so the resur- - } rec - tion of the dead.

8 For as in Adam .... all   —   die : even so in Christ } shall ... ... } all be made a - live.

(GLORIA PATRI.)

2 Dr. Woodward.

3 H. Purcell.

4 Mornington.

5 T. Purcell.

6 GRAND CHANT. P. Humphrey.

7 Dr. Boyce.

Te Deum Laudamus.

J. TURLE.

#								
1	We praise .... Thee,	O	God:	we acknowledge Thee	to	be	the	Lord.
2	All the earth doth...... wor	-	ship Thee:	the Father . .	ev	er	last - — -	ing.
3	To Thee all Angels . . cry	a	-	loud:	the Heavens, and all	the	Powers there -	in.
4	To Thee Cherubim, and Ser	-	a -	phim:	con- — -	. tin -	ual -	ly	do	cry,
5	Holy, . . . Ho	-	ly,	Holy:	Lord . . . God	of	Sa -	ba -	oth;
6	Heaven and earth are } full of the } Ma	-	jes -	ty:	of . . . } Thy	—	Glo -	- ry.
7	The glorious compa- } ny of the Apostles } praise	—	Thee.	the good fellow- } ship of the } Pro	-	phets praise —	Thee.
8	The noble army of } Martyrs } praise	—	Thee.	the Holy Church } throughout all } the world doth } doth	ac -	knowl-edge	Thee;
9	The . . . . Fa	-	—	ther:	of an . . . Infi	-	nite	Ma -	jes -	ty;
10	Thine adorable, true, } and } on	-	ly	Son;	also the Holy . . Ghost,	the	Com -	fort -	er.
11	Thou art the . . King	of	Glory:	O - - -	—	—	Christ.
12	Thou art the ever- - last -	ing	Son:	of . . . —	the	Fa .	—	ther.
13	When Thou tookest } upon Thee to de- } liv	-	er	man:	Thou didst hum- } ble Thyself to } be . . . } born	—	of	a	Virgin.
14	When Thou hadst } overcome the } sharpness of	death:	Thou didst open } the Kingdom } of Heaven to } all	be -	liev -	— -	ers.
15	Thou sittest at the right hand	of	God:	in the . . . Glo	-	ry	of	the	Father.
16	We believe that . . Thou	shalt come:	to . . . be	—	our	—	Judge.
17	We therefore pray Thee, help	Thy servants:	whom Thou } hast redeemed } with	Thy	pre -	cious Blood.
18	Make them to be } numbered } with	Thy Saints:	in . . . Glo	-	ry	ev -	er -	lasting.
19	O Lord, ... save	Thy people:	and . . . bless	Thine her -	i -	tage.
20	Gov- - - . . — - - ern	them:	and . . . lift	them	up	for -	ever.
21	Day . . . —	by	day:	we . . . mag -	ni -	fy	—	Thee;
22	And we . . . worship	Thy Name:	ever, . . . world	with	out	—	end.
23	Vouch- . . - safe,	O	Lord:	to keep us this . day	with -	out	—	sin.
24	O Lord, have mercy up- on	—	us:	have . . . mercy	up -	on	—	us.
25	O Lord, let Thy mercy be	up -	on us:	as our . . . trust	is -	in	—	Thee.
26	O Lord, in Thee . . have	I	trusted:	let me . . . nev -	er	be	con - founded.

9 JOHN ROBINSON.

10 Dr. HODGES.

11 QUADRUPLE CHANT. [To be sung through six times to the 24th verse inclusive.
The 25th and 26th verses taking the last half, as indicated below.]

H. S. OAKELEY.

The 25th verse here.

Benedicite omnia opera Domini.

1st GREGORIAN TONE, 1st ENDING.

	bless	ye the	Lord:	praise Him, and	magni - fy	Him	for - ever.
1 O all ye Works of the Lord,	bless	ye the	Lord:	praise Him, and	magni - fy	Him	for - ever.
2 O ye Angels of the Lord,	"	"	"	"	"	"	"	"
3 O ye Heavens, . .	"	"	"	"	"	"	"	"
4 O ye Waters that be above the Firmament,	"	"	"	"	"	"	"	"
5 O all ye Powers of the Lord,	"	"	"	"	"	"	"	"
6 O ye Sun and Moon,	"	"	"	"	"	"	"	"
7 O ye Stars of Heaven,	"	"	"	"	"	"	"	"
8 O ye Showers and Dew,	"	"	"	"	"	"	"	"
9 O ye Winds of God,	"	"	"	"	"	"	"	"
10 O ye Fire and Heat,	"	"	"	"	"	"	"	"
11 O ye Winter and Summer,	"	"	"	"	"	"	"	"
12 O ye Dews and Frosts,	"	"	"	"	"	"	"	"
13 O ye Frost and Cold,	"	"	"	"	"	"	"	"
14 O ye Ice and Snow,	"	"	"	"	"	"	"	"
15 O ye Nights and Days,	"	"	"	"	"	"	"	"
16 O ye Light and Darkness,	"	"	"	"	"	"	"	"
17 O ye Lightnings and Clouds,	"	"	"	"	"	"	"	"
18 O let the Earth . .	bless	the	Lord : yea, let it	"	"	"	"	"
19 O ye Mountains and Hills,	bless	ye the	Lord :	"	"	"	"	"
20 O all ye Green Things upon the Earth,	"	"	"	"	"	"	"	"
21 O ye Wells, . .	"	"	"	"	"	"	"	"
22 O ye Seas and Floods,	"	"	"	"	"	"	"	"
23 O ye Whales, and all that move in the Waters,	"	"	"	"	"	"	"	"
24 O all ye Fowls of the Air,	"	"	"	"	"	"	"	"
25 O all ye Beasts and Cattle,	"	"	"	"	"	"	"	"
26 O ye Children of Men,	"	"	"	"	"	"	"	"
27 O let Israel, . .	bless	the	Lord :	"	"	"	"	"
28 O ye Priests of the Lord,	bless	ye the	Lord :	"	"	"	"	"
29 O ye Servants of the Lord,	"	"	"	"	"	"	"	"
30 O ye Spirits and Souls of the Righteous,	"	"	"	"	"	"	"	"
31 O ye holy and humble Men of heart,	"	"	"	"	"	"	"	"
Glory be to the Father,	and	to the	Son :	and	to	the Ho - ly	Ghost;
As it was in the beginning, is now, and	ev - er	shall be :	world without	end.	— A - — ·		men.

13

ALFRED BENNETT.

14

15

Dr. W. HAYES.

16

Dr. HODGES.

Jubilate Deo.

17

MACFARREN.

1 O be joyful in the Lord, all ye lands:	serve the Lord with gladness, and come before His . .	pres - ence with a	song.
2 Be ye sure that the Lord He is God :	it is He that hath made us, and not we ourselves ; we are His people, and the	sheep of His —	pasture.
3 O go your way into His gates with thanksgiving, and into His courts with praise:	be thankful unto Him, and	speak good of His	Name.
4 For the Lord is gracious, His mercy is ev - er - lasting:	and His truth endureth from gener - - -	ation to gen - er -	ation.
Glory be to the Father, and to the Son :	and	to the Ho - ly	Ghost.
As it was in the beginning, is now, and ev - er shall be:	world without end. —	A - — -	men.

18

DR. CROTCH.

19

BISHOP MEDLEY.

20

BATTISHILL.

21

DR. JACKSON.
From Walter's "Manual."

Pedal.

22

DR. WOODWARD.

23

NORRIS.

Benedictus.

FARRANT.

1 Blessed be the Lord...	God	of	Israel:	for He hath visited, and	re -	deemed His people;
2 And hath raised up a						
mighty sal- - -	va -	tion for us:		in the house	of	His	ser - vant David;
3 As He spake by the						
mouth of His....	Ho -	ly Prophets:		which have been	since	the	world be - gan;
4 That we should be saved	from	our enemies:		and from the....	hand	of	all	that hate us.
Glory be to the Father,	and	to the Son:		and	to	the	Ho - ly Ghost;
As it was in the be-						
ginning, is now, and	ev -	er shall be:	world without...	end.	—	A - — - men.

25
HINE.

26

27   HANDEL.

28   Dr. BLOW.   **29**   Dr. P. HAYES.

30   JAMES TURLE.

31   **32**   W. H. WALTER. 1867.

Cantate Domino.

RUSSELL.

1 O sing unto the Lord a   new —   song :   for He hath.. ..... done — marvellous things.
2 With His own right } hand, and with His } ho - ly   arm :   hath He.......... gotten Him - self the victory.
3 The Lord declared... His   sal - vation :   His   righteousness hath He openly showed .... } in   the sight of the heathen.

4 He hath remembered } His mercy and truth } toward the .... } house of   Israel :   and all the ends of the } world have seen the }
5 Show yourselves joy- } ful unto the Lord, .. } all   ye   lands :   sal- - - - - - } va - tion   of   our   God.
6 Praise the Lord up- - } on   the   harp :   sing, re- - - - - joice, and give — thanks.
7 With trumpets ...... also and shawms :   sing to the harp with a psalm of thanks- — - giving.

8 Let the sea make a } noise, and all that .. } there - in   is :   O show yourselves } joyful be- - - - } fore the Lord the King.
9 Let the floods clap their } hands, and let the hills } be joyful together be- } fore the Lord :   the round world, and they that dwell there - in.
10 With righteousness } shall He.......... } judge the world :   for He.......... cometh to judge the earth.

Glory be to the Father, and to the Son :   and the.......... peo - ple with — equity.
As it was in the begin- } ning, is now, and .. } ev - er shall be :   and .... to the Ho - ly Ghost;

world without ..... end. — A - — - men.

SAVAGE.

35

36

Hawes.

37

Dr. Jacob Pring.

38

Dr. Hodges.

Bonum est confiteri.

39

BALLAMY.

1 It is a good thing to }
give thanks un- · }   to   the   Lord : || and to sing prais- }
es unto Thy.. } Name, O   Most —   Highest ;

2 To tell of Thy loving }
kindness early.... }   in   the morning : || and of Thy truth   in   the   night — season ;

3 Upon an instrument }
of ten strings, and }
up- · · · · · }   on   the   lute : || upon a loud in- }
strument, ... } and   up - on   the   harp.

4 For Thou, Lord, hast }
made me glad .... } through Thy works : || and I will rejoice }
in giving praise }
for the oper- · } a - tions   of   Thy hands.

Glory be to the Father,   and to the Son : || and .... to   the   Ho - ly   Ghost ;

As it was in the begin- }
ning, is now, and }   ev - er shall be : || world without ... end. — A · — · men.

40

Dr. TURNER.

41

42   Dr. HODGES.

43   Rev. Mr. FITZHERBERT.

Pedal.

44   THOS. ATWOOD.

45   E. HOPKINS.   **46**   LEE.

Deus misereatur.

47

1 God be merciful unto... us, and bless us: and show us the light of His countenance, and be....... merci - ful un - to us:

2 That Thy way may be known upon earth: Thy saving ... health a - mong all nations.
3 Let the people praise... Thee, O God: yea, let .... all the peo - ple praise Thee.
4 O let the nations rejoice and be glad: for Thou shalt judge the folk righteously, and govern the na - tions up - on earth.

5 Let the people praise .. Thee, O God: yea, let .... all the peo - ple praise Thee.
6 Then shall the earth bring .... forth her increase: and God, even our own..... God, shall give us His blessing.

7 God shall .... bless — us: and all the ends of the .... world shall fear ,— Him.

Glory be to the Father, and to the Son: and.......... to the Ho - ly Ghost;
As it was in the beginning, is now, and ev' - er shall be: world without... end. — A - — - men.

48

49   LANGDON.

50   FLINTOFT.

51   GREGORIAN.   52   Dr. ALCOCK.

53   Dr. HODGES.

Benedic, anima mea.

P. PURCELL.

1 Praise the Lord,.....	O	my	soul :	and all that is within me,.............	praise His ho - ly Name.
2 Praise the Lord,.....	O	my	soul :	and for - - - - -	get not all His benefits :
3 Who forgiveth	all	thy	sin :	and healeth all	thine in - fir - mi - ties ;
4 Who saveth thy life..	from	de-struction :		and crowneth thee with	mercy and lov - ing kindness.
6 O praise the Lord, ye Angels of His, ye that ex- - - - - - - -	cel	in strength :		ye that fulfil His commandment, and hearken unto the ..	voice of His — word.
6 O praise the Lord, all ye	His	hosts :		ye servants of	His that do His pleasure.
7 O speak good of the Lord, all ye works of His, in all places of	His	do - minion :		praise thou the	Lord, — O my soul.
Glory be to the Father, and	to the	Son :		and	to the Ho - ly Ghost ;
As it was in the be- ginning, is now, and	ev -	er shall be :		world without	end. — A - — - men.

Dr. P. HAYES.

56
Rev. Wm. Jacons.

57
Rev. W. H. Havergal.

58
Dean Aldrich

59
Orlando Gibbons.

Burial of the Dead.

60 BURIAL CHANT.

1 Lord, let me know mine end, and the number of my days : that I may be certified how .... long I have to live.

2 Behold, Thou hast made my days as it were a span long, and mine age is even as nothing in re- - - - - spect of Thee: and verily every man living is.......... al - to - geth - er vanity.

3 For man walketh in a vain shadow, and dis-quieteth him- - - - self in vain : he heapeth up riches, and cannot tell .... who shall gath - er them.

4 And now, Lord, what is my hope: Truly my .... hope is even in Thee.

5 Deliver me from all.. mine of - fences : and make me not a re- buke un - to the foolish.

6 When Thou with re-bukes dost chasten man for sin, Thou makest his beauty to consume away, like as it were a moth..... fretting a garment: every man.......... there - fore is but vanity.

7 Hear my prayer, O Lord, and with Thine ears con- - - - - sider my calling : hold not Thy .... peace — at my tears.

8 For I am a .... stran-ger with Thee: and a sojourner, as all my fa - thers were.

9 O spare me a little, that I may re- - - cover my strenth : before I go hence,... and be no more seen.

10 Lord, Thou hast been our refuge : from one gener- - - a - tion to an - other.

11 Before the mountains were brought forth, or ever the earth and the world were made : Thou art God from everlasting, and ... world with - out — end.

12 Thou turnest man .. to de-struction: again Thou sayest, Come a- - - - - gain, ye children of men.

13 For a thousand years in Thy sight are ... but as yesterday: seeing that is past .. as a watch in the night.

14 As soon as Thou scatterest them, they are even............... as a - sleep: and fade away ...... sudden-ly like the grass.

15 In the morning it is green, and .... grow - eth up : but in the evening it is cut down, ... dri - ed up, and withered.

16 For we consume away in Thy dis-pleasure: and are afraid at Thy wrath - ful in - dig - nation.

17 and our secret sins in the light — of Thy countenance.

18 For when Thou art angry, all our ..... days are gone: we bring our years to an end, as it....... were a tale that is told.

19 The days of our age are threescore years and ten; and though men be so strong that they come to ...... four - score years: yet is their strength then but labour and sorrow; so soon pass-eth it a- - - - - way, and we are gone.

20 So teach us to ...... number our days : that we may apply our hearts — un - to wisdom.

(GLORI PATRI.)

61   "I HEARD A VOICE FROM HEAVEN."   Dyce.

I heard a voice from Heaven, saying un - to me, Write, From henceforth blessed are the dead who............ die in the Lord:

Even so....... saith the Spir - it; for they rest..... from their la - - bours.

62   "THY WILL BE DONE."   Rev. A. H. D. Troyte.

A - men.

1 My God, my Father, while I stray,
Far from my home, in life's rough way,
O teach me from my heart to say,
    " Thy will be done."

2 Though dark my path, and sad my lot,
Let me be still and murmur not,
Or breathe the prayer divinely taught,
    " Thy will be done."

3 What though in lonely grief I sigh
For friends beloved no longer nigh,
Submissive would I still reply,
    " Thy will be done."

4 If Thou should'st call me to resign
What most I prize, it ne'er was mine ;
I only yield Thee what is Thine ;
    " Thy will be done."

5 Let but my fainting heart be blest
With Thy sweet Spirit for its guest,
My God, to Thee I leave the rest ;
    " Thy will be done."

6 Renew my will from day to day,
Blend it with Thine, and take away
All that now makes it hard to say,
    " Thy will be done."   Amen.

For other appropriate Hymns, see Nos. 62, 96, 101 and 102.

63   OLD 100th. L. M. Doxology.

Attributed to G. Franc.
1543.

Praise God, from Whom all bless - ings flow; Praise Him, all crea - tures here be - low;

Praise Him a - bove, an - gel - ic host; Praise Father, Son, and Ho - ly Ghost. A - men.

64   EVENING HYMN. L. M. Hymn 168.

TALLIS.
Dr. Hodges' Collection.

1 Glo - ry to Thee, my God, this night, For all the bless - ings of the light;
2 For - give me, Lord, for Thy dear Son, The ills that I this day have done;
3 Teach me to live, that I may dread The grave as lit - tle as my bed;

Keep me, O keep me, King of kings, Un - der Thine own Al - mighty wings.
That with the world, my-self, and Thee, I, ere I sleep, at peace may be.
Teach me to die, that so I may Tri - umphing rise at the last day. A - men.

65   ATTLEBOROUGH. L. M. HYMN 94.   Dr. WAINWRIGHT. ob. 1800.

1 My God, and is Thy ta - ble spread, And does Thy cup with love o'er-flow?
2 Hail, sa - cred feast, which Je - sus makes, Rich ban - quet of His Flesh and Blood!

Thi - ther be all Thy children led, And let them Thy sweet mer - cies know.
Thrice hap-py he who here partakes That sa - cred stream, that heavenly food. A - men.

66   TRINITY. L. M. HYMN 77.   MARTIN LUTHER. 1543.
Arranged by Dr. W. H. WALTER.

1 O Ho - ly, Ho - ly, Ho - ly Lord, Bright in Thy deeds, and in Thy Name,
2 O Je - sus, Lamb once cru - ci - fied To take our load of sins a - way,
3 O Ho - ly Spir - it from a - bove, In streams of light and glo - ry given,

For - ev - er be Thy Name a - dored; Thy glo - ries let the world proclaim.
Thine be the hymn that rolls its tide A - long the realms of up - per day.
Thou source of ec - sta - cy and love, Thy prais - es ring thro' earth and heaven. A - men.

67 HURSLEY. L. M. Hymn 268. GERMAN.

1 Sun of my soul, Thou Sa - viour dear, It is not night if Thou be near;
2 When the soft dews of kind - ly sleep My wearied eye - lids gent - ly steep,
3 A - bide with me from morn till eve, For without Thee I can - not live;

O may no earth - born cloud a - rise To hide Thee from Thy ser - vant's eyes.
Be my last thought how sweet to rest For ev - er on my Saviour's breast.
A - bide with me when night is nigh, For without Thee I dare not die. A - men.

68 ROCKINGHAM. L. M. Selection 38. DR. MILLER.

1 Let me with light and truth be bless'd; Be these my guides to lead the way,
2 Then will I there fresh al - tars raise To God, Who is my on - ly joy;
3 Why then cast down, my soul? and why So much oppressed with anx - ious care?

Till on Thy ho - ly hill I rest, And in Thy sa-cred tem - ple pray.
And well-tuned harps, with songs of praise, Shall all my grateful hours em - ploy.
On God, thy God, for aid re - ly, Who will thy ruined state re - pair. A-men.

69 BOWEN. L. M. Selection 57.

HAYDN.
Dr. Hodges' Collection.

1 Thy presence, Lord, hath me sup - plied, Thou my right hand sup - port dost give;
2 Whom then in heaven, but Thee a - lone, Have I, whose fa - vour I re - quire?
3 My trembling flesh and ach - ing heart May oft-en fail to suc - cour me;

Thou first shalt with Thy coun - sel guide, And then to glo - ry me re-ceive.
Throughout the spacious earth there's none, Compared with Thee that I de - sire.
But God shall in - ward strength im - part, And my e - ter - nal por - tion be. A-men.

70 GRACE CHURCH. L. M. Hymn 39.

PLEYEL.

1 Al - might - y Fa - ther, bless the word, Which through Thy grace we now have heard;
2 We praise Thee for the means of grace, Thus in Thy courts to seek Thy Face:

O may the precious seed take root, Spring up, and bear a - bun - dant fruit.
Grant, Lord, that we who wor - ship here, May all, at length, in heaven ap - pear. A - men.

71   VENI, CREATOR SPIRITUS.

THE PRESIDING BISHOP.   THE BISHOPS, WITH OTHERS PRESENT.

Come, Ho - ly Ghost, our souls in - spire,	And light - en with ce - les - tial fire.
Thou the an-oint - ing Spir - it art,	Who dost Thy seven - fold gifts im - part.
Thy bless - ed unc - tion from a - bove,	Is com - fort, life, and fire of love.
En - a - ble with per - pet - ual light	The dul - ness of our blind - ed sight.
An - oint and cheer our soil - ed face	With the a - bundance of Thy grace.
Keep far our foes, give peace at home;	Where Thou art guide, no ill can come.
Teach us to know the Fa - ther, Son,	And Thee, of Both, to be but One.
That, through the a - ges all a - long,	This may be our end - less song;

FULL CHORUS.

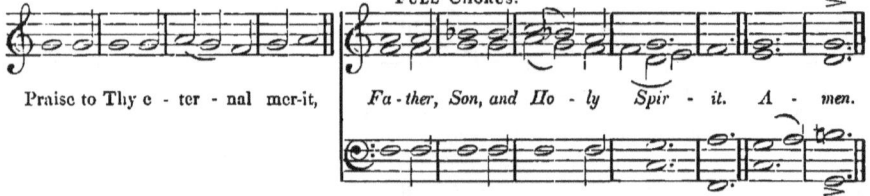

Praise to Thy e - ter - nal mer-it,   Fa - ther, Son, and Ho - ly Spir - it. A - men.

72   CHRISTMAS. C. M.   HYMN 180.

HANDEL.
Dr. Hodges' Collection.

1 A - wake, my soul, stretch ev' - ry nerve, And press with vigour on;   A heavenly race de-
2 A cloud of wit - ness - es a - round Hold thee in full sur - vey;   For - get the steps al-
3 'Tis God's all an - i - mat-ing voice That calls thee from on high,   'Tis His own hand pre-

mands thy zeal, And an im - mor - tal crown, And an im - mor-tal crown.
read - y trod, And on - ward urge thy way, And on - ward urge thy way.
sents the prize To thine up - lift - ed eye, To thine up - lift - ed eye. A-men.

73 DUNDEE. C. M. SELECTION 18. Scotch Psalter. 1615.

1 The Lord Him - self, tho - might - y Lord, Vouchsafes to be my guide;
2 In ten - der grass He makes me feed, And gent - ly there re - pose;
3 He does my wandering soul re - claim, And, to His end - less praise,

The Shepherd, by Whose con - stant care My wants are all sup - plied.
Then leads me to cool shades, and where Re - fresh - ing wa - ter flows.
In - struct with hum - ble zeal to walk In His most righteous ways. A - men.

74 ST. PETER. C. M. SELECTION 21. REINAGLE. 1860.

1 Judge me, O Lord, for I the paths Of right - eous - ness have trod;
2 I'll wash my hands in in - no - cence, And round Thine Al - tar go;
3 My thanks I'll pub - lish there, and tell How Thy re - nown ex - cels;

I shall not fail, who all my trust Re - pose on Thee, my God.
Pour the glad hymn of tri - umph thence, And thence Thy won - ders show.
That seat af - fords me most de - light, In which Thine hon - our dwells. A - men.

75 LONDON NEW. C. M. Hymn 12.

1 God moves in a mys - te - rious way His won - ders to per - form;
2 Deep in un - fath - om - a - ble mines, With nev - er - fail - ing skill,
4 Judge not the Lord by fee - ble sense, But trust Him for His grace;

He plants His footsteps in the sea, And rides up - on the storm.
He treasures up His bright de - signs, And works His gra - cious will.
Be - hind a frown-ing prov - i - dence He hides a smil - ing face. A - men.

76 ST. ANN. C. M. Selection 108.
Dr. Croft. 1703.

1. Bless God, ye ser - vants, that at - tend Up - on His sol - emn state;
2. With - in His house, lift up your hands, And bless His ho - ly Name;

That in His tem - ple's hal - low'd courts With hum - ble reverence wait.
From Si - on bless Thy Is - rael, Lord, Who earth and heaven didst frame. A - men.

77   BELMONT. C. M. Hymn 10.   MOZART.

1 When all Thy mer - cies,   O   my   God,   My   ris - ing soul sur - veys,
11 Through ev - 'ry   pe - riod   of   my   life   Thy   good-ness I'll   pur - sue ;
13 Through all e - ter - ni - ty, to   Thee   A   joy - ful   song I'll raise;

Transport - ed with the view, I'm lost In won - der, love, and praise.
And af - ter death, in dis - tant worlds, The glo - rious theme re - new.
But O !   e - ter - ni - ty's too short To ut - ter all Thy praise. A - men.

78   TIVERTON. C. M. Selection 95.   GRIGG.

1 With cheer - ful notes let all the earth To heaven their voi - ces raise ;
2 God's ten - der mer - cy knows no bound, His truth shall ne'er de - cay ;

Let all, inspired with god - ly mirth, Sing sol - emn hymns of praise.
Then let the wil - ling na - tions round Their grate - ful tri - bute pay. A - men.

79 WINDSOR. C. M. SELECTION 115.　　KIRBY. 1592.

```
1 Lord, hear my prayer, and to my cry    Thy  wont-ed  au-dience  lend;
2 Nor at Thy strict tri-bu-nal bring      Thy  ser-vant  to  be  tried;
3 To Thee my hands in hum-ble prayer      I  fer-vent-ly  stretch  out;
```

```
In Thy ac-cus-tom'd faith and truth   A   gra-cious an-swer  send.
For in Thy sight no liv-ing man        Can  e'er be jus-ti-fied.
My soul for Thy re-fresh-ment thirsts, Like land op-press'd with drought. A-men.
```

80 ST. STEPHEN. C. M. SELECTION 29.　　Rev. WM. JONES. ob. 1800.

```
1 Through all the chang-ing scenes of life, In    trou-ble and  in   joy,
3 O     mag-ni-fy the  Lord with me,       With  me ex-alt His Name:
4 The   An-gel of the   Lord en-camps      A-round the good and  just;
```

```
The prais-es of my God shall still My heart and tongue em-ploy.
When in dis-tress to Him I call'd, He  to  my res-cue came.
De-liv-'rance He af-fords to all Who on His suc-cour trust. A-men.
```

81   ST. JAMES.   C. M.   Hymn 170.   COURTEVILLE. 1680.

1 Now from the al - tar of our hearts, Let flames of love a - rise;
2 Min - utes and mer - cies mul - ti - plied Have made up all this day;
3 New time, new fa - vours, and new joys, Do a new song re - quire;

As - sist us, Lord, to of - fer up Our even - ing sac - ri - fice.
Min - utes came quick, but mer - cies were More swift, more free than they.
Till we shall praise Thee as we would, Ac - cept our heart's de - sire. A - men.

82   NORTHAMPTON.   C. M.   Hymn 209.   Dr. CROFT. 1709.

1 Thou art the Way; to Thee a - lone From sin and death we flee;
2 Thou art the Truth, Thy word a - lone True wis - dom can im - part;
3 Thou art the Life; The rend - ing tomb Pro-claims Thy conquering arm,
4 Thou art the Way, the Truth, the Life; Grant us that Way to know,

And he, who would the Fa - ther seek, Must seek Him, Lord, by Thee.
Thou on - ly canst in - form the mind, And pu - ri - fy the heart.
And those who put their trust in Thee, Nor death nor hell shall harm.
That Truth to keep, that Life to win, Whose joys e - ter - nal flow. A - men.

83   MORAVIA. S. M. Hymn 88.   MORAVIAN. 1770.

1 Sol - diers of Christ, a - rise,   And put your ar - mour on,
2 Strong in the Lord of Hosts,   And in His migh - ty power,
3 Stand then in His great might,   With all His strength en - dued;
4 That hav - ing all things done,   And all your con - flicts past,

Strong in the strength which God supplies Through His e - ter - nal Son.
Who in the strength of Je - sus trusts Is more than con - quer - or.
And take, to arm you for the fight, Tha pan - o - ply of God.
Ye may be - hold your victo - ry won, And stand com - plete at last. A - men.

84   ST. BRIDE. S. M. Selection 44.   DR. HOWARD. 1770.

1 Have mer - cy, Lord, on me,   As Thou wert ev - er kind;
2 Wash off my foul of - fence,   And cleanse me from my sin;
10 The joy Thy fa - vour gives   Let me, O Lord, re - gain;

Let me, op - press'd with loads of guilt, Thy wont - ed mer - cy find.
For I con - fess my crime, and see How great my guilt has been.
And Thy free Spir - it's firm sup - port My faint - ing soul sus - tain. A - men.

85 ST. AUGUSTINE. S. M. Hymn 25.

1 I love Thy king-dom, Lord, The house of Thine a - bode,
2 I love Thy Church, O God; Her walls be - fore Thee stand,
5 For her my tears shall fall; For her my prayers as - cend;

The Church our blest Re - deem - er saved With His own pre - cious Blood.
Dear as the ap - ple of Thine eye, And gra - ven on Thy hand.
To her my cares and toils be given, Till toils and cares shall end. A - men.

86 CAMBRIDGE. S. M. Selection 52.

Rev. R. Harrison.

1 To bless Thy cho - sen race, In mer - cy, Lord, in - - cline;
2 That so Thy wondrous way May through the world be known;
3 Let differing na - tions join To cel - e - brate Thy fame;

And cause the brightness of Thy Face On all Thy Saints to shine.
While dis - tant lands their tri - bute pay, And Thy sal - va - tion own.
Let all the world, O Lord, combine To praise Thy glo - rious Name. A - men.

87 NETLEY. S. M. Double. HYMN 176.

MORAVIAN.

1 Je - - sus, my Strength, my Hope, On Thee I cast my care,
2 I want a so - ber mind, A self - re - nounc - ing will,

With hum - ble con - fi - dence look up, And know Thou hear'st my prayer;
That tram - ples down, and casts be - hind The baits of pleas - ing ill:

Give me on Thee to wait, Till I can all things do;
A soul in - ured to pain, To hard - ship, grief, and loss,

On Thee, Al - might - y to cre - ate, Al - might - y to re - new.
Read - y to take up and sus - tain The con - se - cra - ted Cross. A - men.

88 INNSPRUCK. II. 1. HYMN 28.

German Choral. 1490.
From J. S. BACH.

1 { With joy shall I be - hold the day, That calls my will - ing soul a - way,
  { For lo! my great Re - deem - er's power Un - folds the ev - er - last ing door,
2 { Ev'n now, to my ex - pect - ing eyes The heaven-built towers of Sa - lem rise;
  { I view her man-sions that con - tain The an - gel host, a beauteous train,

1st time.   2nd time.

To dwell a - mong the blest: And points me to His rest.
Their glo - ry I sur - vey; And shine with cloud - less day. A - men.

89 DARWELL. II. 4. SELECTION 122.

Rev. J. DARWELL.

1 Ye boundless realms of joy, Ex - alt your Maker's fame; His praise your song employ A-bove the
2 Thou moon, that rul'st the night,And sun that guid'st the day, Ye glittering stars of light. To Him your
3 Let them a - dore the Lord, And praise His Ho-ly Name, By whose Almighty word They all from

star - ry frame: Your voices raise, Ye Cheru-bim And Seraphim, To sing His praise.
homage pay: His praise declare, Ye heavens above, And clouds that move In liquid air.
nothing came; And all shall last From changes free; His firm decree Stands ever fast. A - men.

1 God is our ref - uge in dis - tress, A pres - ent help when dan - gers press,

In Him, un-daunt - ed, we'll con - fide; Though earth were from her cen - tre tost,

And moun-tains in the o - cean lost, Torn piece - meal by the roar - ing tide. A-men.

2 A gentler stream with gladness still
  The city of our Lord shall fill,
    The royal seat of God most high :
  God dwells in Sion, whose fair towers
  Shall mock th' assaults of earthly powers,
    While His Almighty aid is nigh.

3 Submit to God's Almighty sway,
  For Him the Heathen shall obey,
    And earth her sovereign Lord confess :
  The God of Hosts conducts our arms,
  Our tower of refuge in alarms,
    As to our fathers in distress.

91 "THE LORD MY PASTURE SHALL PREPARE." II. 3. Hymn 9.

MOZART.
Arranged by Dr. JOHN H. WILLCOX.

1 The Lord my pas - ture shall pre - pare, And feed me with a shep - herd's care;

His presence shall my wants sup - ply, And guard me with a watch-ful eye;

My noon-day walks He shall at - tend, And all my midnight hours de - fend. A - men.

2 When in the sultry glebe I faint,
Or on the thirsty mountain pant,
To fertile vales and dewy meads
My weary wandering steps He leads,
Where peaceful rivers, soft and slow,
Amid the verdant landscape flow.

3 Though in the paths of death I tread,
With gloomy horrors overspread;
My steadfast heart shall fear no ill,
For Thou, O Lord, art with me still:
Thy friendly crook shall give me aid,
And guide me through the dreadful shade.

92 RUSSIAN HYMN. P. 5. Hymn 53.

Dr. Hodges' Collection.

1 Rise,crown'd with light,im-perial Sa-lem, rise; Ex-alt Thy towering head, and lift Thine eyes:
2 See a long race Thy spacious courts a-dorn, See fu-ture sons, and daughters yet un-born,
3 See barbarous na-tions at Thy gates attend, Walk in Thy light, and in Thy tem-ple bend:
4 The seas shall waste, the skies to smoke decay, Rocks fall to dust, and mountains melt a-way;

See heaven its sparkling portals wide display, And break up-on thee in a flood of day.
In crowding ranks on eve-ry side a-rise, De-mand-ing life, im-patient for the skies.
See Thy bright Altars thronged with prostrate kings, While eve-ry land its joyous tribute brings.
But fixed His word, His saving power remains; Thy realm shall last, Thy own Mes-si-ah reigns. A-men.

93 EVENTIDE. P. 5. Hymn 264.

W. H. Monk.

1 A-bide with me! fast falls the e-ven-tide, The darkness deepens; Lord, with me a-bide;
2 Swift to its close ebbs out life's little day; Earth's joys grow dim, its glories pass a-way;
5 Hold Thou Thy Cross before my closing eyes; Shine thro' the gloom, and point me to the skies;

When other helpers fail, and comforts flee, Help of the helpless, O a-bide with me.
Change and decay on all around I see; O Thou who changest not, abide with me.
Heaven's morning breaks, and earth's vain shadows flee; In life, in death, O Lord, abide with me. A-men.

94 "BRIEF LIFE IS HERE OUR PORTION." II. 6. Hymn 275.

S. Salvatori.

1 Brief life is here our por - tion, Brief sor - row, short - lived care;
2 And now we fight the bat - tle, But then shall wear the crown
3 O sweet and bless - ed coun - try, The Home of God's e - lect!

The life that knows no end - ing, The tear - less life is there.
Of full and ev - er - last - ing And pas - sion - less re - nown
O sweet and bless - ed coun - try, That ea - ger hearts ex - pect!

O hap - py re - tri - bu - tion! Short toil, e - ter - nal rest:
The morn - ing shall a - wak - en, The sha - dows pass a - way,
Je - sus, in mer - cy bring us To that dear land of rest;

For mor - tals and for sin - ners, A man - sion with the blest.
And each true - heart - ed ser - vant Shall shine as doth the day.
Who art, with God the Fa - ther, And Spir - it ev - er blessed. A - men.

95 "JERUSALEM THE GOLDEN." II. 6. HYMN 276.

ALEXANDER EWING.

1 Je - ru - sa - lem, the gold - en! With milk and hon - ey blest;
2 They stand, those halls of Si - on, All ju - bi - lant with song,
3 And they, who with their Lead - er Have conquered in the fight;

Be - neath Thy con - tem - pla - tion Sink heart and voice op - prest.
And bright with many an an - gel, And all the mar - tyr throng.
For ev - er, and for - ev - er, Are clad in robes of white.

I know not, Oh! I know not What joys a - wait me there;
There is the throne of Da - vid, And there, from toil re - leased,
O land that seest no sor - row! O state that fear'st no strife!

What ra - dian - cy of glo - ry, What bliss be - yond com - pare.
The shout of them that triumph, The song of them that feast.
O roy - al land of flow - ers! O realm and home of life! A - men.

(Doxology, 3d verse of Hymn 275, No. 94.)

1 { Great God, what do I see and hear! The end of things cre - a - - ted ! }
{ The Judge of man I see ap - pear, On clouds of glo - ry seat - ed : }

4 { Great God, what do I see and hear! The end of things cre - a - - ted ! }
{ The Judge of man I see ap - pear, On clouds of glo - ry seat - ed : }

The trum - pet sounds ; the graves re - store The dead, which they contained be - fore:

Be - neath His Cross I view the day, When heaven and earth shall pass a - way,

Pre - - pare, my soul, to meet Him.

And thus pre - pare to meet Him. A - men.

2 The dead in Christ shall first arise,
   At the last trumpet's sounding,
Caught up to meet Him in the skies,
   With joy their Lord surrounding :
No gloomy fears their souls dismay ;
His presence sheds eternal day
   On those prepared to meet Him.

3 But sinners, filled with guilty fears,
   Behold His wrath prevailing ;
For they shall rise, and find their tears
   And sighs are unavailing :
The day of grace is passed and gone ;
Trembling they stand before the throne,
   All unprepared to meet Him.

97 LITANY. III. 1. Hymn 56.   Richard Redhead.

1 Sa - viour, when in dust, to Thee, Low we bow the ador - ing knee;
O, by all Thy pains and woe, Suf - fered once for man be - low,

When, re - pent - ant, to the skies, Scarce we lift our streaming eyes; }
Bend - ing from Thy throne on high, Hear our sol - emn lit - a - ny. } A - men.

98 INNOCENTS. III. 1. Hymn 155.   Old Litany.

1 Songs of praise the an - gels sang; Heaven with Al - le - lu - ias rang,
2 Songs of praise a - woke the morn, When the Prince of Peace was born;
3 Heaven and earth must pass a - way; Songs of praise shall crown that day:
4 And shall man a - lone be dumb, Till that glo - rious king - dom come?

When Je - ho - vah's work be - gun, When He spake, and it was done.
Songs of praise a - rose, when He Cap - tive, led cap - tiv - i - ty.
God will make new heavens and earth; Songs of praise shall hail their birth.
No; the Church de - lights to raise Psalms, and hymns, and songs of praise. A - men.

99 VIENNA. III. 1. SELECTION 105. KNECHT. 1792.

1 Lord, for ev - er at Thy side Let my place and por - tion be:
2 Meek - ly may my soul re - ceive All Thy Spir - it hath re - vealed;
3 Hum - ble as a lit - tle child, Wean - ed from the moth - er's breast,
4 Is - rael! now and ev - er - more In the Lord Je - ho - vah trust;

Strip me of the robe of pride, Clothe me with hu - mil - i - ty.
Thou hast spo - ken—I be - lieve, Though the or - a - cle be sealed.
By no sub - tle - ties be - guiled, On Thy faith - ful word I rest.
Him, in all His ways, a - dore, Wise, and won - der - ful, and just. A - men.

100 EASTER HYMN. III. 1. HYMN 69. W. H. MONK.

{ Christ, the Lord, is risen to - day, }
{ Sons of men and angels say: } Al - le - lu - ia. Raise your joys and triumphs high; Al-le - lu - ia.

Sing, ye heavens, and, earth, re - ply. Al - le - lu - ia. A - men.

1 Je - sus, Sa - viour of my soul, Let me to Thy Bo - som fly,
2 Oth - er re - fuge have I none; Hangs my help - less soul on Thee:

While the waves of trou - ble roll, While the tem - pest still is high:
Leave, ah! leave me not a - lone; Still sup - port and com - fort me:

Hide me, O my Sa - viour, hide, Till the storm of life is passed;
All my trust on Thee is stayed, All my hope from Thee I bring;

Safe in - to the ha - ven guide; O re - ceive my soul at last.
Cov - er my de - fence-less head With the shad - ow of Thy wing. A - men.

RICHARD REDHEAD.

1 Rock of a - ges, cleft for me, Let me hide my - self in Thee:
2 Should my tears for - ev - er flow, Should my zeal no lan - guor know;

Let the Wa - ter and the Blood, From Thy Side, a heal - ing flood,
This for sin could not a - tone; Thou must save, and Thou a - lone:

Be of sin the dou - ble cure, Save from wrath, and make me pure.
In my hand no price I bring, Sim - ply to Thy Cross I cling. A - men.

3 While I draw this fleeting breath,
  When mine eye-lids close in death,
  When I rise to worlds unknown,
  And behold Thee on thy throne,—
  Rocks of ages, cleft for me,
  Let me hide myself in Thee.

4 Praise the Name of God most high,
  Praise Him all below the sky,
  Praise Him all ye heavenly host,
  Father, Son, and Holy Ghost;
  As through countless ages past,
  Evermore His praise shall last. Amen.

103 SHARON. III. 3. SELECTION 70. PART II.

Dr. Boyce.
Dr. Hodges' Collection.

1 God shall charge His an - gel le - gions Watch and ward o'er thee to keep;
3 Since, with pure and firm af - fec - tion, Thou on God hast set thy love,
4 Thou shalt call on Him in trou - ble, He will heark - en, He will save;

Though thou walk through hostile re - gions, Though in des - ert wilds thou sleep.
With the wings of His pro - tec - tion He will shield thee from a - bove.
Here for grief re - ward thee double, Crown with life be - yond the grave, A - men.

104 BATTY. III. 3. HYMN 18.

German.

1 Sa - viour, source of eve - ry bless - ing, Tune my heart to grate - ful lays;
2 Teach me some me - lo - di - ous measure, Sung by rap - tured saints a - bove;
3 Thou didst seek me when a stranger, Wandering from the fold of God;
4 By Thy hand re - stored, de - fend - ed, Safe through life thus far I've come;

Streams of mer - cy, nev - er ceas-ing, Call for cease - less songs of praise.
Fill my soul with sa cred pleasure, While I sing re - deem - ing love.
Thou to save my soul from dan - ger, Didst re - deem me with Thy Blood.
Safe, O Lord, when life is end - ed, Bring me to my heaven-ly home. A - men.

105 AUSTRIA. III. 3. DOUBLE. HYMN 150. HAYDN.

1 Lord, with glow - ing heart, I'd praise Thee, For the bliss Thy love be - stows,
For the pard'ning grace that saves me, And the peace that from it flows:
Help, O God, my weak en - deav - our; This dull soul to rap - ture raise:
Thou must light the flame, or nev - er Can my love be warmed to praise. A-men.

2 Praise, my soul, the God that sought thee,
Wretched wanderer, far astray,
Found thee, lost, and kindly brought thee
From the paths of death away :
Praise, with love's devoutest feeling,
Him who saw thy guilt-born fear,
And, the light of hope revealing,
Bade the blood-stained Cross appear.

3 Lord, this bosom's ardent feeling
Vainly would my lips express :
Low before Thy footstool kneeling,
Deign Thy suppliant's prayer to bless :
Let Thy grace, my soul's chief treasure,
Love's pure flame within me raise ;
And, since words can never measure,
Let my life show forth Thy praise.

106 "HE IS RISEN." III. 4. HYMN FOR EASTER. J. NEANDER. 1610.

1 He is ris - en, He is ris - en! Tell it with a joy - ful voice,
2 Come, ye sad and fear - ful heart - ed, With glad smile and ra - diant brow;

He has burst His three days' pris - on, Let the whole wide earth re - joice:
Lent's long shad - ows have de - part - ed, All His woes are o - ver now;

Death is con - quer'd, man is free, Christ has won the vic - to - ry.
And the pas - sion that He bore, Sin and pain, can vex no more. A - men.

3 Come, with high and holy hymning,
Chant our Lord's triumphant lay ;
Not one darksome cloud is dimming
Yonder glorious morning ray,
Breaking o'er the purple East ;
Brighter far our Easter feast.

4 He is risen, He is risen !
He has oped th'eternal gate ;
We are free from sin's dark prison,
Risen to a holier state ;
And a brighter Easter beam
On our longing eyes shall stream.

107 SICILY. III. 5. Hymn 40. or III. 3, by omitting the repeat.

Italian Melody.

1 { Lord, dis - miss us with Thy bless - ing, Fill our hearts with joy and peace; }
  { Let us, each Thy love pos - sess - ing, Tri - umph in re - deem - ing grace: }
2 { Thanks we give, and a - do - ra - tion, For the Gos - pel's joy - ful sound; }
  { May the fruits of Thy sal - va - tion In our hearts and lives a - bound: }

O re - fresh us; O re - fresh us, Trav'l-ling through this wil - der - ness!
May Thy pres - ence, May Thy pres - ence With us ev - er - more be found. A - men.

108 HANOVER. IV. 1. SELECTION 123.

Dr. CROFT. 1699.

1 O praise ye the Lord, Prepare your glad voice, His praise in the great As - sem - bly to sing :
2 Let them His great Name Ex-tol in their songs, With hearts well attuned His prais-es ex - press;
3 With glo - ry adorn'd, His people shall sing To God, Who their heads With safety doth shield;

In their great Crea - tor Let Israel re - joice ; And children of Si - on Be glad in their King.
Who always takes pleasure To hear their glad tongues, And waits with salvation The humble to bless.
Such honour and triumph His favour shall bring ; O therefore, for ev-er All praise to Him yield. A - men.

109   ST. ANDREW. IV. 2. HYMN 173.

1 In - spir - er   and Hear - er   of   prayer, Thou Shepherd   and Guardian   of Thine,
2 If   Thou art   my Shield and   my   Sun,   The   night is   no dark - ness   to   me;
3 A   Sovereign Pro - tect - or   I   have,   Un - seen, yet   for ev - er   at hand;
4 His smiles and   His com - forts   a - bound, His   grace, as   the dew, shall   de - scend;

My   all to   Thy cov - e - nant   care,   I, sleeping or waking,   re - sign.
And, fast as   my minutes roll   on,   They bring me but near - er   to Thee.
Un - change-a - bly faith-ful to   save,   Al - might-y   to   rule and command.
And walls of sal - va - tion sur - round The soul He   de - lights to de - fend.   A-men.

110   WESTBROOK. IV. 3. HYMN 153.

1 Be   joy - ful in God, all   ye lands of the earth, O serve Him with gladness and fear;
2 For Je - ho - vah is God, and Je - ho - vah a - lone, Cre - a - tor and Ru - ler o'er all;
3 O   en - ter His gates with thanksgiving and song, Your vows in His tem-ple proclaim;

Ex - ult in His presence with mu - sic and mirth, With love and de - vo - tion draw near.
And we are His peo - ple, His sceptre   we own; His sheep, and we fol - low His call.
His praise with me - lo-dious ac - cordance prolong, And bless His a - do - ra - ble Name. A-men.

111 "ADESTE, FIDELES." IV. 4. Doxology. John Reading. 1680.

Come, let us adore Him; Come, bow at His Feet; O give Him the glo-ry, the praise that is meet;

Let joyful Ho-san-nas un-ceas-ing a - rise, And join the full chorus that gladdens the skies,

And join the full cho - rus that glad - dens the skies. A - men.

112 HYMN CHANT. Hymn 152. Wood.

1 { The God of Abra-ham praise, Who reigns en-throned a-bove; Ancient of ever - last - ing days, And God of love;
{ Jehovah, Great I AM, By earth and heaven confess'd: I bow and bless the sacred Name For ever bless'd.
2 { The God of Abra-ham praise, At Whose su - preme command From earth I rise, and seek the joys At His right Hand.
{ I all on earth for - sake, Its wisdom, fame, and power; And Him my only portion make, My Shield and Tower.
6 { The whole tri-umphant host Give thanks to God on high; "Hail, Father, Son, and Ho-ly Ghost," They ever cry:
{ Hail, Abraham's God and mine, I join the heav'n - ly lays; All might and majes-ty are Thine, And endless praise.

A - men.

113 TYNEMOUTH. Hymn 145. MORAVIAN.

1 Rise, my soul, and stretch thy wings; Thy bet - ter por - tion trace;
2 Cease, my soul, O! cease to mourn; Press on - ward to the prize;

Rise, from tran - si - to - ry things, Towards heaven, thy des - tined place:
Soon thy Sa - viour will re - turn, To take thee to the skies:

Sun, and moon, and stars de - cay, Time shall soon this earth re - move;
There is ev - er - last - ing peace, Rest, en - dur - ing rest, in heaven;

Rise, my soul, and haste a - way, To seats prepared a - bove.
There will sor - row ev - er cease, And crowns of joy be given. A - men.

www.ingramcontent.com/pod-product-compliance
Lightning Source LLC
Chambersburg PA
CBHW021523090426
42739CB00007B/760